Mr Bridgman's Accomplice

Long Ben's Coxswain

Mr Bridgman's Accomplice

First Published in 2019 by FastPrint Publishing Peterborough, England.

A CIP catalogue record for this book is available from the British Library

Paperback ISBN 978-178456-636-4

Printed and bound in England by www.printondemand-worldwide.com

www.fast-print.net/bookshop

Mr Bridgman's Accomplice

Long Ben's Coxswain
1660 - 1722

John Dann

"We turned the Fancy from the wind and ran out 40 guns..."

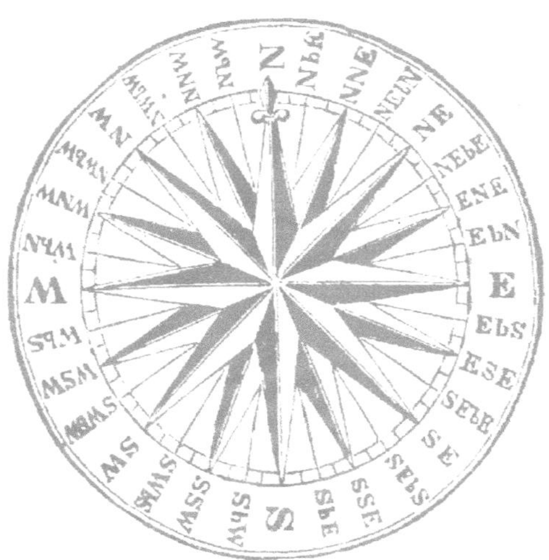

Contents

"...And soon the sky was filled with smoke that hid us from the sun..."

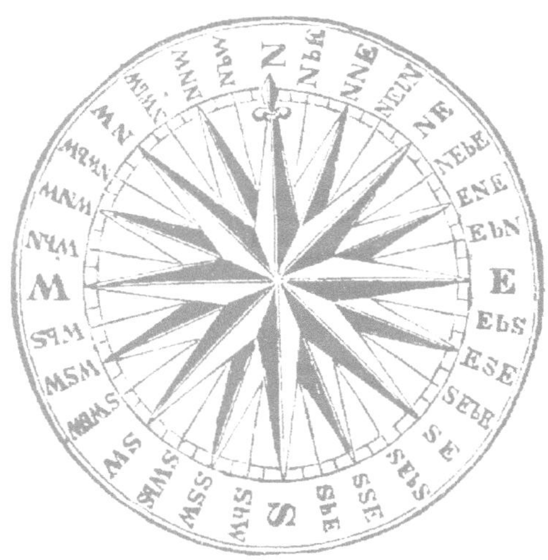

Preface

Whilst researching family history I stumbled upon an interesting ancestor with the same name -a first cousin five times removed. This is not uncommon in the paternal line, but what was unusual was his involvement in *The Pitkin Affair* a little known but well documented cause célèbre in early eighteenth century London.

Even better, I also discovered that in an earlier life he had taken part in one of the most notorious pirate raids in history, led by Henry Every. It was the talk of mercantile London.

Parliament declared the pirates *hostis humani generis* (enemies of the human race), issued a £500 bounty and when the East India Company later doubled that reward (astronomical at the time), the first worldwide manhunt in recorded history was underway.

In charting his progress through the 'golden age' of piracy, (c.1660-c.1730) it was necessary to occasionally speculate with small factual jig-saw pieces to form a mostly true story narrative. However any interpretations of events and characterisation together with any mistakes are mine alone.

Adventurers have something in common, a willingness to take risks – ordinary people who did extraordinary things.

JD

"…Then up and down the ship we fought, until the decks ran red…"

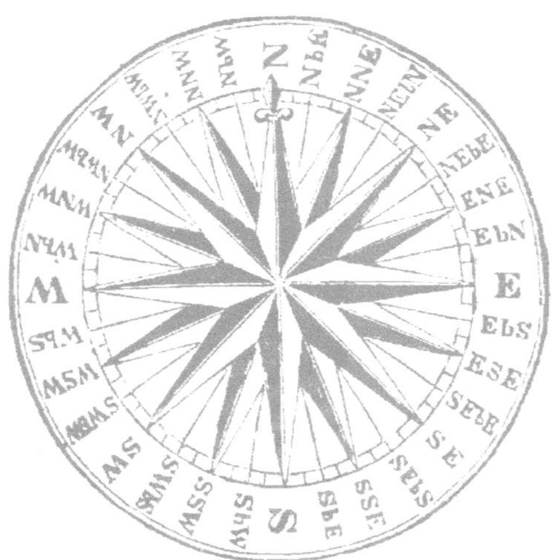

-1-
The smuggler

"Them that ask no questions isn't told a lie"

"If you meet King George's men, dressed in blue and red,
You be careful what you say, and mindful what is said.
If they call you 'pretty maid', and chuck you 'neath the chin,
Don't you tell where no one is, nor yet where no one's been!

If you do as you've been told, 'likely there's a chance,
You'll be give a dainty doll, all the way from France,
With a cup of Valenciennes, and a velvet hood –
A present from the Gentlemen, along 'o being good!
Five and twenty ponies
Trotting through the dark…"

'A smugglers song', by Rudyard Kipling who lived in Sussex

England was in the last throws of civil war. After his defeat at the battle of Worcester in September 1651, King Charles II was on the run through Southern England. For many weeks, he was hidden by supporters in 'safe houses' managing to evade pursuers. In October the King escaped from Sussex, carried safely across the channel from Shoreham to the French port of Fécamp in Captain Tattersall's coal-brig the *Surprise*. It had such a profound effect that on his restoration Charles purchased the ship and re- named her *HMY Royal Escape*.

The next ten years saw a puritanical Commonwealth government under the Lord Protector Cromwell. After his death the English Parliament agreed to restore the exiled King Charles II. He entered London on 29 May 1660, popularly known as Oak Apple Day.

Around the same year John Dann was born in East Hoathly a village in the Sussex Weald. He was the only son of Thomas Dann and Mary Repose. Mary came from Broomfield Kent and a record shows John was baptised 28 August 1662 in her home village.

East Hoathly Parish Church

Halland House once the Pelham family home

East Hoathly is a small village, eight miles north-east from Lewes. Another eight miles to the west is Heathfield, located on an ancient trackway called the Ridgeway, connecting the South Downs with the Weald. Its market charter was granted in 1316 during the reign of Edward II.

During John's youth the iron industry had brought prosperity to the Heathfield area and provided local employment. Iron had been crudely smelted here since Roman times with forest charcoal used in the process, as well as for domestic fuel. There were ironworks here in 1574 when ordnance and shot were supplied to Elizabethan forces, a route through East Hoathly passing Sir Nicholas Pelham's Halland house to the Lewes garrison.

England was still in turmoil in his early childhood - there had been a Great Plague in London when he was five followed a year later by the Great Fire, but his family had remained relatively safe in the Sussex countryside.

At sea we were at war with the Dutch whose navy had sailed up the river Medway and destroyed the English fleet and captured *HMS Royal Charles.* The demands of these wars meant that extra revenue was raised by imposing Excise Duty on certain goods manufactured in the country, such as candles and beer. These detested taxes on items in daily use had the overall effect of doubling or even trebling their cost.

It was clearly to the advantage of everyone except the government, to smuggle such items into the country if they could, free of tax. But it was the restrictions on the export of English wool which had the greatest impact. In an attempt to protect our cloth industry, it was made illegal to export wool from other than designated ports, and for some years after 1662 this was a capital (hanging) offence. This restriction was particularly irksome to wool producers on the Sussex downs and coastal marshes and led predictably to widespread flouting of the restrictions. It was said that many thousand packs of wool per year were being shipped out illegally from Kent and Sussex, within days of a shearing.

The 'Owling trade', was the common term for smuggling sheep or wool from England to another country, particularly France. The practice was illegal in England from the fourteenth century. Participants were called 'owlers', their ships 'owling boats'. The lonely Romney Marshes became the centre of smuggling and by the 1670s something like twenty thousand packs of wool were illegally sent to Calais annually. The smugglers were now building fast and armed sloops ships (the French called them shallops) to carry out their nocturnal runs.

These were often controlled by Huguenot families -French Protestants who had fled to England a century earlier as refugees from religious persecution, after the St Bartholomew's Day Massacre in Paris in August 1572.

Rye was a natural destination being the largest port in Sussex in the late sixteenth century and the Royal Mail route to Europe. Besides, religious non-conformity had existed in Rye and nearby communities before the Reformation thanks to the Lollards, followers of John Wycliffe, who wanted to reform the Catholic Church. Protestants even managed to take control of the Rye Corporation. Many Huguenots returned home when civil and religious freedom was restored by the Edict of Nantes in 1598, but in the seventeenth century the tide turned against Protestants once more and refugees again fled from persecution.

As much as half of Rye's population at the time were of Huguenots extraction. Those who came included prosperous merchants and skilled craftsmen, with a strong work ethic, who were welcomed and considered beneficial to the town. Huguenots were to make important contributions as doctors, wig making, shoemakers, goldsmiths and weavers, and not to mention their continental contacts.

The continental clothiers conspired with the English wool producers to ensure that the trade continued, and cargoes of Lyons silk, Valenciennes lace and brandy were shipped back in part-payment for the prized high quality wool.

John's father died when he was ten, leaving the family near destitute. Most villagers knew someone involved in the 'Owling trade'; and this is how he was recruited into the smugglers network -or 'Free Traders' as they preferred to call themselves. He would learn his trade as a boy-sailor on board one of their sloops. This was a high risk business, but *"them that ask no questions…"* could earn much more that a farm labourer or working in the ironworks.

He was able to support his mother and sisters as the Owling trade offered something like twelve pence a day. It expanded into the import of luxury goods from the Continent. Silks, tea, tobacco and brandy were profitable items to bring in to evade the heavy duties imposed by the Government. To combat this, Charles II had established the Board of Customs in 1671 and by 1685 there were ten ships (smacks) patrolling the coast between Yarmouth and Bristol.

A certain William Carter lamented *"that the misery of England was the great quantity of wool stolen out of England".* [1] Holland received whole ship-loads of wool from Ireland, besides what was being stolen from the Kentish, Essex, and Sussex coasts.

The Romney Marsh men were not only content with the exportation of their own growth, but also sought wool up to ten or twenty miles in-land, bringing it to the sea-shore, for continental shipment. All attempts at effective prosecution of the offenders were defeated. [2]

"If you wake at midnight, and hear a horse's feet,
Don't go drawing back the blind, or looking in the street.
Them that ask no questions isn't told a lie.
Watch the wall, my darling, while the Gentlemen go by!
Five and twenty ponies,
Trotting through the dark -
Brandy for the Parson,
'Baccy for the Clerk;
Laces for a lady, letters for a spy,
And watch the wall, my darling, while the Gentlemen go by!"

After the Glorious Revolution, the death penalty for felony was thought too severe, as very few convictions had taken place under it. In reality of course despite all the effort of the authorities, the coast men had set the law at defiance. They openly carried their wool at shearing-time, on pack-horses to the sea-shore, where French vessels were ready to receive it and attacked fiercely anyone who ventured to interfere.

The same William Carter, a local clothier with a vested interest, had been conducting virtually a 'one-man' war against the owlers, was sharply attacked in 1688. Having procured the necessary warrants, seized eight or ten men on Romney Marsh, who were carrying the wool on pack-horses to be shipped. He requested the Mayor of Romney to commit them. Possibly in the pay of the owlers or wishing to live a peaceful life among his neighbours the mayor admitted them to bail instead. In the meantime, Carter and his assistants retired to *George Inn* in Lydd a few miles away, but had to flee the next day pursued by a large group of armed horsemen. So fast was the pursuit when they arrived at Camber Point they could not manage their horses over Guldeford ferry; so they abandoned them. Luckily, some ships' boats gave assistance, and the riders got safely into Rye. One witness commented "*...had they not got into the boats, Mr. Carter would have received some hurt, for many of the exporters were desperate fellows, not caring what mischief they did.*" [3] Despite all, the illicit exportation of wool was never stopped.

War with France

Over the centuries the navy consistently suffered manpower shortages due to the low pay and a lack of qualified seamen. Impressment was first made lawful during Elizabethan times, though it had been a common practice of drafting soldiers dating back to the thirteenth century.

In 1563 Queen Elizabeth passed '*an Act touching politick considerations for the maintenance of the Navy*' which defined more clearly the liability of sailors who may be forced to serve as mariners. It was taken further in 1597 when the *Vagrancy Act* was passed, which now allowed for men of disrepute to be impressed for service in the fleet.

During a period of war there would be an increased demand and the navy forced unwilling individuals into service. Usually they would take place at sea, easier to secure able seamen by boarding merchant ships, ransacking their men and often leaving them without sufficient hands to take them safely into port. However, residents of seaports also lived in fear of the press gangs that patrolled waterfronts and raided taverns, pouncing on deserters and idle mariners.

This is where John experienced the first of his misadventures – that would ironically lead to new opportunities. The owlers had been flaunting the authorities for years, and often relaxed at coastal inns enjoying the benefits of their import-export business. Possibly in collusion with, or as a result of a tip off by the aggrieved William Carter, an unfortunate event took place in the winter of 1688-9 at the *Mermaid Inn* in Rye. The pub was unexpectedly visited by the 'Impress Service' and he found himself 'press-ganged' into the navy, despite there being a secret escape tunnel leading to the *Old Bell Inn,* in the adjacent street. Records show a group of thirty-two men and a boy - 'eligible men of seafaring habits between the ages of 18 and 55 years' were sent to Chatham on the King's service to man the King's ships. [4]

War had broken out against the French in September 1688 in what became known as the Nine Years' War (1688–97), fought between King Louis XIV of France, and a coalition, led by the English and Dutch. The following year a Bill was passed in Parliament banning all trade with France, provoking a riot in Rye.

John was now coxswain on *HMS Soldado*, originally built as Her Majesty's yacht - *HMY Suadadoes* for Catherine of Braganza, wife of Charles II. It had been re-built as a sixteen-gun fire-ship, commanded by John Graydon, as part of the English Squadron. His first engagement was the *Battle of Bantry Bay* fought in May 1689. Although outnumbered, and despite no loss of ships the English fleet still incurred over three-hundred casualties, the outcome remained somewhat inconclusive.

At much the same time Henry Every, a west countryman, also known to contempories as John Avery [5] was serving as chief mate on the sixty-four-gun vessel *HMS Rupert.* The ship took part in another encounter, known as the *Battle of Beachy Head* off the coast of Sussex in the English Channel a year later in July 1690.

Three years later their paths would cross when in 1693 John had deserted the *Soldado* for an opportunity to take part in what promised to be a profitable expedition to the West Indies. But fate intervened and instead he was to join Henry Every in a very different venture.

Mermaid Inn Rye

The battle of Bantry Bay May 1689

-2-

The pirate

"... and bound to seek our fortunes"

John was arrested for suspected piracy on Friday morning 27 July 1696, in Rochester Kent. He had travelled from London by coach the previous day, staying at the *Bull hotel* in the High Street.

Whilst away from his room, a curious maid became suspicious of the weight of his jacket, alerted the mayor, and collected a (£10) reward in the process. He was committed to custody and the jacket confiscated. Quilted into the lining, he has secreted over a £1,000 in gold and silver coins, about £165,800 in today's money.

A week later on Friday 3 August, in order to avoid the possibility of execution, he agreed to testify against captured members of Captain Henry Every's crew, considered the most notorious pirate of his time.

As piracy was a capital crime, and the death penalty could only be handed down if there were eyewitnesses, the testimony of Dann's examination was crucial.

18th century engraving, Henry Every with the Fancy

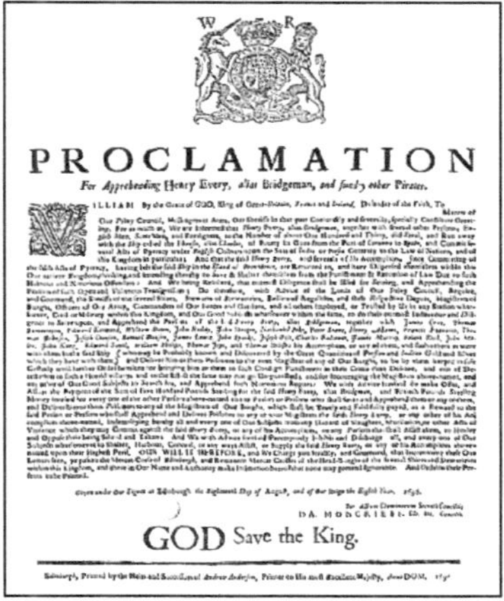

W R

PROCLAMATION

For Apprehending Henry Every, alias Bridgeman, and sundry other Pirates.

GOD Save the King.

Proclamation to apprehend Henry Every (1696) a £500 reward for Every and a fiftieth (£10) for his accomplices

The story had started three years earlier in the spring of 1693 when John was Coxswain of the prize fire-ship *Soldado.* He deserted and signed on to the *James* –one of four ships, including *Charles II* (flagship), *Dove* and *Seventh Son,* that had been assembled by London-based investors; led by Sir James Houblon, a wealthy merchant hoping to reinvigorate the stagnating English economy. Known as the Spanish Expedition, the ships were to prey on French vessels in the West Indies, under an arrangement with the Spanish. They were to sail to La Coruña in Northern Spain, to await payment. Whilst at anchor John had moved to the privateer *Charles II*. Time drifted, and unrest set in amongst crews, by now had something like eight months' pay due, and no prospects of settlement. One evening in May 1694 whilst Captain Gibson was alone in his cabin, most of the crew of *Charles II* mutinied. Events had been inspired by Henry Every, the ship's first mate, and duly elected the new captain, with John Dann as coxswain. After putting Gibson and a few non-conspirators in a pinnace, they set sail renaming the ship *Fancy*.

With a course set south for Madagascar, the *Fancy* captured three English merchantmen at the Cape Verde islands, later robbing two Danish vessels near São Tomé and Príncipe in October, the first acts of piracy by Every and his crew. Sailing around the Cape of Good Hope they arrived at the island of Johanna (Anjouan) in the Comoros Islands, where Every had the *Fancy* careened –running her ashore on a sandy beach for cleaning, caulking, and repair. On 18 February 1695, he left a message for passing sea captains which reads:

> *"…that Fancy, man of war, formerly the Charles of the 'Spanish Expedition' who departed from La Coruña 7th May 1694, being then and now a ship of 46 guns, 150 men and bound to seek our fortunes."* [6]

It was known that a wealthy flotilla returning from an annual pilgrimage to Mecca would pass through the narrow Straights of Bab-el-Mandeb, simply known as the 'Babs' to the pirates, separating the Red Sea from the Gulf of Aden. Arriving in June 1695 at Bob's Key (now Perim), a small island in the straits, Every began preparing their ambush. He joined forces with five other pirate captains, with similar plans - Thomas Tew of the *Amity*, Joseph Faro, *Portsmouth Adventure*, Richard Want, *Dolphin*, William Mace of the *Pearl* and Thomas Wake of the *Susanna*. The latter two, held colonial privateering commissions from Governor Fletcher of New York and Rhode Island. *Fancy* being the largest ship, Every was elected admiral of this formidable pirate flotilla – six ships with a total of over 400 pirates. It was weeks of waiting.

Then after questioning an Arab trader, they learned the Mughal ships had already sailed –giving them the slip in the darkness, so they made haste to intercept them. After four or five days sailing, four of the flotilla were unable to keep up –leaving the faster *Fancy* and *Pearl* to encounter the Mughal treasure convoy. On 5 September, they sighted it off the coast of India in the straights of Surat. It including the 1,600 ton flagship *Ganj-i-sawai*, a massive behemoth, with eighty cannon, loaded to the brim with treasure along with the 600 ton *Fateh Muhammed* as escort.

The *Fancy* gave chase and with little resistance boarded the *Fateh Muhammed* installing a prize crew. Continuing the chase managed to overtake the *Ganj-i-Sawai*, and with a lucky shot snapped its mainmast in a cannonball volley. Losing leeway, unable to escape there followed several hours of ferocious hand-to-hand combat on deck, with the pirates emerging victorious. Although many pirates were reportedly killed, the payoff was astonishing. Every, had captured up to £600,000 in gold and silver coins, precious jewels, silks and ivory (tens of millions in today's terms) making him the richest pirate in the world. It has subsequently been called as the most profitable pirate raid in history.

In response to Every's attack on the Mughal convoy, a combined bounty of £1,000 (considered massive by the standards of the time) was offered for his capture by the Privy Council and East India Company, leading to the first worldwide manhunt in recorded history.

He sailed to Bourbon Island (Réunion) to share the spoils, and continued to the Caribbean sailing for New Providence (Bahamas) arriving in April 1696. It was a known pirate haven, with a bribable Governor, Nicholas Trott. [7] Every was now in his forties, described as *"a tall, strongly built man"* known as 'Long Ben' to his crewmen and associates. He had begun using the alias Benjamin or Henry Bridgman since arriving in the Bahamas. He and his crew lived aboard the *Fancy,* even though they had given her to the Governor as part of the bribe. However, the ship was driven ashore in a gale, and after salvaging her guns and whatever else they could, the pirates dispersed. Some made their way to the American colonies, successful bribing Governor Markham of Philadelphia, whilst another nineteen of Every's crew clubbed together to purchase a ship called the *Isaac* and made the voyage across the Atlantic, to Achill, Westport and Galway on the south west coast of Ireland. A few weeks later in June, Every and the remaining twenty-five crew members including his coxswain John Dann, now a close companion, made a similar voyage in the *Sea Flower* a sloop of 50 tons and 4 guns. During the Atlantic crossing the wife of Henry Adams the ship's gunner and quartermaster seems to have changed her affections and taken up with Henry Every. The ship arrived in late June at Dunfanaghy on the north coast of Ireland in county Donegal.

Every bribed Maurice Cuttle an unscrupulous port official, for passes to allow John and others to travel to Dublin and from there the crew parted company. Every's whereabouts and activities after this period are speculative, as he managed to elude capture. John made his way to Londonderry and from there to Dublin where he spent a few days meeting up with old shipmates at the *Wooden Man Tavern* in Temple Bar (*now The Norseman*) just a stroll from Wood Quay.

Their presence caused something of a stir due to the large sums of money being spent. After some arrests were made, John decided to take passage to England with fellow crew mate Thomas Johnson the ship's cook. They sailed to Holyhead and took the mail coach to Chester parting company at the *White Lion hotel.* The following day John continued alone towards London, a journey taking four days.

White Hart Inn St Albans

The Swan with Two Necks, Lad lane (Gresham Street)

On the third day he arrived at the *White Hart Inn* on Holywell Hill St Albans, meeting by chance Mrs Adams as she was about to enter another coach. She was the estranged wife of Henry the *Fancy's* quartermaster, who had been listed on the Government's pirate proclamation. Explaining she was on her way to meet Captain Bridgman, (Every's adopted name), but would not reveal his whereabouts. However she gave him details of a trusted and discreet Huguenot émigré in London – by the name of Madame Harache.

He finally arrived in London towards the end of July, the coach delivering its passengers to the *Swan with Two Necks*, in Lad lane (now Gresham Street) off Wood Street. At this time London was the second largest city in Europe with a population of half a million people. London's trade was flourishing with the colonies, and goldsmiths were becoming more involved with this finance.

The White Bear Piccadilly

Courtyard of the Bull hotel Rochester

The next day John made his way to Great Suffolk Street, to meet with Madame Harache. Anne and her husband Pierre were members of a wider and well-connected Huguenot family. He had known many such families in the past from his 'owling days' in Sussex. Some had settled in Rye, whilst others after fleeing had moved to London, and the Low Countries. The Harache's arrived in England from Rouen fifteen years earlier and established themselves as goldsmiths. Unusual for the time, Anne was a practicing goldsmith in her own right. She was well established having recently supplied silver plate to Charles Seymour, sixth Duke of Somerset for Petworth House in Sussex.

John had left some gold coins and gemstones for safekeeping. This was a welcome addition, because coin supply at the time had become erratic –leading to the re-coinage act the same year. Anne advised him to take passage to the Continent, selling the remaining amount through their network where silver yielded a higher bullion price.

Perhaps with thoughts of home, without news of his mother or sisters, John may have decided to visit East Hoathly before travelling to the Low Countries. So at five the next morning he left by coach from the *White Bear Inn* (now the *Criterion Theatre* in Piccadilly), arriving at the *Bull hotel* in the Kent port of Rochester.

However this is where his luck ran out - he was arrested. Whilst away from his room, a suspicious maid (possibly an informer) had found his jacket extremely heavy, (it would have weighed at least eight pounds) discovering gold coins quilted into the lining, said to contain 1,045 sequins and 10 Guineas. On his return he was detained, brought before the Mayor and imprisoned. His jacket and remaining fortune was subsequently lost to the authorities.

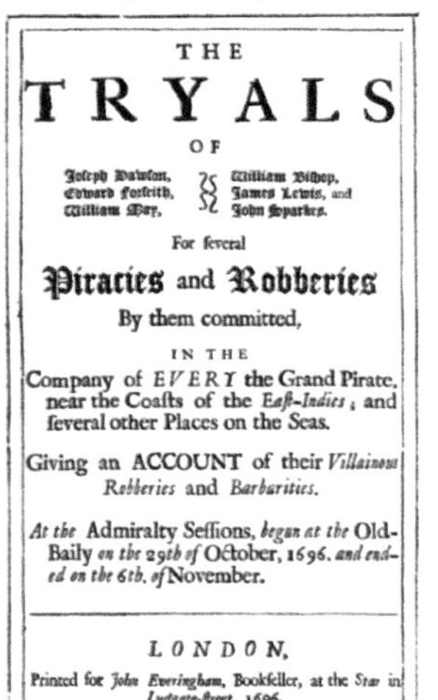

THE

TRYALS

OF

Joſeph Dawſon, Edward Forſeith, William May, William Biſhop, James Lewis, and John Sparkes.

For ſeveral

Piracies and Robberies

By them committed,

IN THE

Company of *EVERY* the Grand Pirate, near the Coaſts of the *Eaſt-Indies*; and ſeveral other Places on the Seas.

Giving an ACCOUNT of their *Villainous Robberies* and *Barbarities*.

At the Admiralty Seſſions, *began at the* Old-Baily *on the 29th of* October, 1696. *and ended on the 6th. of* November.

LONDON,

Printed for *John Everingham*, Bookſeller, at the *Star* in *Ludgate-ſtreet*, 1696.

Faced with death, he decided to cooperate, escaping the hangman by turning Kings Evidence. The 'Examination of John Dann, Mariner', was taken Friday 3 August 1696. [8] The subsequent pirate trial at the Old Bailey in London created considerable public excitement. In October 1696 six of the captured crew members of the *Fancy* were tried at the Old Bailey in London. The original trial acquitted them, much to the dismay of the authorities. However they were re-tried the next month under a different charge and six sentenced to death, although Joseph Dawson was reprieved the remaining five were hanged at Execution Dock Wapping on 25 November 1696. At the trial Dann's testament together with fellow crew member Phillip Middleton [9] was decisive. Middleton had been a boy at the beginning of *Fancy's* cruise, and just thirteen-year-old at the trial. After the second trial in November John had been pardoned. By the New Year he had slipped back into anonymity taking temporary lodgings amongst old ship-mates in Wapping or Ratcliffe, known as 'Sailor Town,' the location of shipbuilders, ship-owners, captains, merchants and crew since Elizabethan times. Many sailors' wives ran alehouses, and shops, earning a living whilst their men were at sea.

For example Every's wife Anne, was a periwig seller in the Ratcliffe Highway, and under surveillance. With the hue and cry, she must have been resigned to the fact he would have been betrayed for the reward if he ever visited or sent word.

A ballard had been written about Every's exploits and no doubt John enjoyed a drink or two toasting 'old Long Ben'.

'We turned the Fancy from the wind and ran out 40 guns
And soon the sky was filled with smoke that hid us from the sun
Then up and down the ship we fought, until the decks ran red
And when the fight was done we drank and this is what we said,
Chorus:
Here's to gentlemen at sea tonight, and a toast to all free men
And when the devil comes to take us home, he'll drink
With old Long Ben!"

Eighteen months later he was summoned by Robert Blackborne the secretary of the East India Company, to appear on August 11 1698 before the board, at East India House Leadenhall Street to give testament. *"John Dann, seaman, gave information as to his voyage with Every in the Fancy, from Corunna to the Guinea coast, where they took ships with forty pound weight of gold-dust, thence round the Cape to Madagascar, where they victualled, thence to the …Red Sea, where they took a large ship, … thence to the Bahamas, where they paid 2,500 pieces of eight to Governor Trott, and dispersed. Every brought home £2,000; Dann and others £500 or £600 apiece."* [10]

John clearly under-estimated the real haul, no doubt under pressure from the East India Company who had a vested interest in a lower amount as they had to provide compensation. For his consideration John received £1,300 principal shares in the company under the alias of Francis Danne. [11]

Old East India House c1680

Some years had now elapsed - it was time for John to leave the sea and play another part. With the help of his Huguenot friends (and what remained of his loot) he was to seek another but legitimate fortune, but first to learn about the business of goldsmith banking.

-3-
The goldsmith banker
... at the sign of the King's Head, in the Strand

London in the 1660s was one of the largest cities in the world. Thanks to its status as a hub of global trade, combined with its role as the seat of government, it had developed a relatively sophisticated money market. The city's goldsmiths soon became part of this growing financial network. Their businesses flourished as the development of international trade boosted available supplies of gold.

Many of them branched out into accepting clients' valuables for safe keeping in their vaults. They began to make payments on behalf of clients, on the basis of the precious items lodged with them, thus gradually evolving into bankers.

By the 1670s there were 44 such 'goldsmith bankers' in London. Pierre Harache, the first Huguenot goldsmith to be admitted to the Goldsmiths' Company in Foster Lane, was able to introduce John to many members. Some carried on an extensive bullion and bills of exchange business with the continent. In the earlier part of the century they had often handled plate and silver captured from Spanish ships.

John Coggs was a well-established and respected Goldsmith Banker who traded from the sign of the *Kings Head*, in the Strand close to St Clements church. He was married with two children. We are told that he introduced customer pass-books [12], an innovative arrangement used by banks. Previously, it was customary for depositors to call regularly and check up their accounts.

He had opened his shop in 1662 soon after the restoration of King Charles II and had developed a reputation for reliability and caution. He offering running cashes for some of his clients (lending money they held as deposits), and operated a clearing account at Blanchard & Childs.

The banks clients included some notable people such as Sir John Holt, the Lord Chief Justice, as well as members of the aristocracy like the Duke of Marlborough, and others with family connections to King James, such as the Earl of Rochester, one time Lord Treasurer, Earl of Litchfield, Earl of Deloraine a Scottish peer and the Earl of Ailesbury.

John Coggs's house on Belsize estate Middlesex 1696

St Botolph Bishopsgate 1796

John Coggs business flourished, and by 1683 he had taken a house on the Belsize estate off Haverstock Hill, set in parkland. It was fashionable with prosperous merchants and others who wanted a country house within easy reach of London. Now a banker of prominence in the City, he re-built the house in 1686 and commissioned an oil painting by the Flemish landscape artist *Jan Siberechts* which now hangs in the Tate Gallery London.

Charles Holloway, who had a similar goldsmith business close by at Temple Bar, had joined him in 1692, creating *Coggs and Holloway.* Coggs's wife Martha died in January 1696, and by the summer he was acting as banker for the new Hospital for Seamen in Greenwich. In 1699, his partner dying, and himself elderly and unwell; through the bona fides of the Harache connection Coggs took John Dann into the business forming yet another partnership *Coggs and Dann.*

Now integrated into London's mercantile society, the following year John married Elizabeth a mature woman in her mid-thirties, daughter of Nathaniel Noble of Stonesby, a small Leicestershire village near Melton Mowbray. Known as Eliza, she had inherited property in Leicester, and a sizable sum from her late Aunt, Mary Williamson, now living in the London parish of St Alban Wood Street. They married on 14 January 1700 at St Botolph-without-Bishopsgate, one of the few London churches to have survived the great fire of 1666. They lived comfortably amongst Mercers, Lacemen and merchant traders, in Henrietta Street Covent Garden. They celebrated their status, by commissioning modest sized portraits by a Dutch artist *Pieter van der Werff* then visiting London.

Around this time, Thomas Brerewood a well-connected 'gentleman' draper began keeping a running account with *Coggs and Dann*, whose shop in the Strand was near his house on Norfolk Street. Brerewood was also a clever con man with a persuasive manner; it was to prove fateful. In February 1705 a massive bankruptcy fraud was discovered involving Brerewood and his co-conspirator Thomas Pitkin which was to shake London. Although they were quickly caught, unravelling the fraud was very complicated required three large insolvencies, four acts of Parliament and lasted for years.

Brerewood had negotiated primarily with John who was less experienced than old Mr Coggs. Who was now happy to leave many transactions to Dann, devoting much of his time sitting on the board of *St Clement Danes* Pauper Settlements and Parish Vestries.

This probably explains how the firm became so involved in this disadvantageous affair. The problem was that Brerewood after securing further loans was now over £49,000 in debt to his bankers, more money than he could pay. *Coggs and Dann* realized they could not save their business.

On 12 January 1710, the bankers gave notice to their creditors in the *Post Man*; newspaper, that they had become insolvent and would stop all payments. Trustees were appointed to unravel the extent of the debts as there were over 200 creditors. John Coggs, now an elderly widower, whose long career as a trusted banker had ended in ruins, died in March the same year. [13] His son John junior, continued independently as a goldsmith from the 1720s till his death in 1751. [14]

Two years later, the Government introduced the *'Coggs' and Dann's Bill'* [15] in an attempt to speed up payment to creditors. Still, the complexity of the fraud took over forty years to resolve, only the subsequent 'South Sea bubble' of 1721 was greater.

Whilst some *Coggs and Dann* creditors chose anonymity, the identity of others gives a vivid sense of how significant the bank's failure was. The list of proved debts ran to 217 names and totalling over £54,000. One such creditor John Holt, as Chief Justice of the King's Bench was one of the presiding judges in the pirate trial at the Old Bailey where Dann in a previous life gave evidence. One wonders if he ever made the connection? In 1703 he had ruled in Coggs's favour in the landmark case for English property and contract law in *Coggs v Bernard.*

Sir John Holt, Lord Chief Justice (1642–1710) £500

John Churchill, 1st Duke of Marlborough (1650–1722) £1,268

John Holles, 1st Duke of Newcastle (1662 –1711) £1,570

Thomas Howard, 8th Duke of Norfolk, (1683–1732) £872

Edward Henry Lee, 1st Earl of Lichfield (1663–1716)

Major-General Henry Scott, 1st Earl of Deloraine, (1676–1730) £5,919

Dann was astute enough to cooperate with the bank's trustees and commissioners over the years in liquidating the bank's assets. These included creditors, Sir James How (owed £29), Lord Shelbourne (£137) and Lord Lanesborough (£2,100).

John's wife Eliza had also written to another trustee William Draper (owed £3,104), to plead for some leniency as she had her own dowry income and property in Leicester to protect:

> *"I am sorry to heare by Mr Dann [that] ye trustees will not be so kind as to give me some small consideration, for my ioyning in ye conveyance of his house att lester, but [that] I must be obliged to do it, and trust to what theay shall please to do for me afterwards; all though [that] concern is but small to ye cred[itors] yet in case I Should survive Mr Dann, it might be of some help to me, considering I have lost my all by him, and not admitted as one of his creditors, nor any ways provided for by him, but however S[ir] in hopes I maye enioye ye goods I now posses, and that Mr Dann maye have faver*

shewne him by you & ye rest of ye trustees, as to what I understand by him, he has humbly requested; I will be ready upon a dayes notice, to go with any person you shall please to appoint before a Judge, so that theare may be no furder delaye in [that] afaire upon my account." [16]

Presumably the trustees did show Dann favour, for he received small payments from time to time from the estate. Although John and Eliza had by now discretely moved to more modest lodgings in Theobald's Court, it appears the wily couple still maintained some wealth.

Sir Francis Child, of the bankers Child & Co. in Fleet Street, *(now part of the Royal Bank of Scotland Group)*, took over most of the business, using the upper-storey rooms in the Temple Bar for their records storage. The complexity of the fraud was only finally resolved around 1747, years after Dann had died. In the 1850s its believed the bank was the model for Charles Dicken's fictitious Tellson's Bank*.

John died on 22 August 1722 and buried in St Andrew's Holborn -the same church John Coggs was interred twelve years earlier. Probate dated 20 September revealed his simple wishes, requesting funeral expenses and debts be paid as soon as possible. He left no specific bequests, named no property, and as they were childless, merely left his entire estate to Eliza his sole executrix.

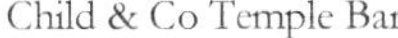

Child & Co Temple Bar

St Andrew's Church Holborn Hill London

Within a few months Elizabeth too had died. She wrote a detailed will on 5 November and died on 28 December. The Prerogative Court of Canterbury Wills probate show she left substantial amounts, £100 each to her brother Daniel, and her married sister, various other relatives and a god-daughter, all together over £650, something like £93,000 today. Amongst her bequests were some portraits, household china, a diamond ring, other jewellery and personal items, together with an amount of £30 for her funeral expenses. She was buried in St. Dunstan in-the-West.

* Features in *A Tale of Two Cities*, 1859

With her death, properties and contents sold - and having no heirs this branch of the Dann family was neatly pruned.

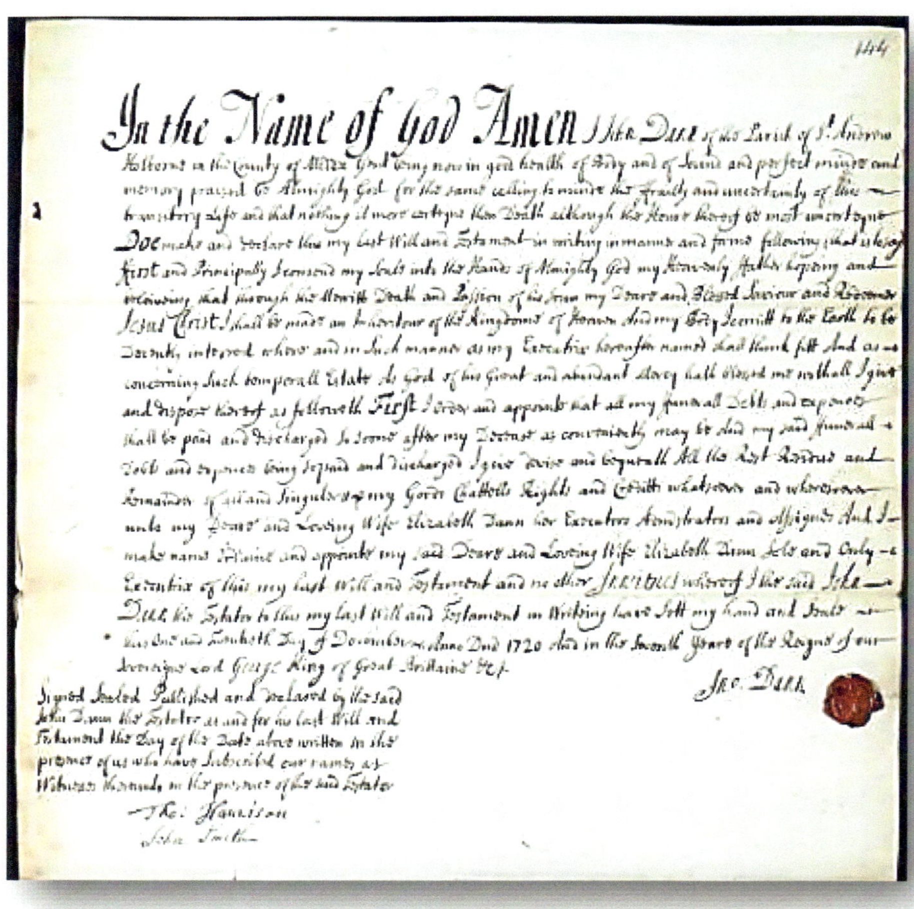

144

In the Name of God Amen I John Dann of the Parish of St. Andrew Holborn in the County of Middx Gent being now in good health of Body and of Sound and perfect mind and memory praised be Almighty God for the same calling to mind the frailty and uncertainty of this transitory life and that nothing is more certaine than Death although the Houre thereof be most uncertaine Doe make and declare this my last Will and Testament in writing in manner and forme following (that is to say) First and Principally I commend my Soule into the Hands of Almighty God my Heavenly Father hoping and beleiving that through the Meritts Death and Passion of his Sonn my Deare and Blessed Saviour and Redeemer Jesus Christ I shall be made an Inheritour of the Kingdome of Heaven And my Body I committ to the Earth to be decently interred where and in such manner as my Executrix hereafter named shall think fitt And as concerning such temporall Estate as God of his Great and abundant Mercy hath blessed me withall I give and dispose thereof as followeth First I order and appoint that all my funerall Debts and expences shall be paid and discharged so soone after my decease as conveniently may be And my said funerall Debts and expences being so paid and discharged I give devise and bequeath All the Rest Residue and Remainder of all and singular my Goods Chattells Rights and Credits whatsoever and wheresoever unto my Deare and Loving Wife Elizabeth Dann her Executors Administrators and Assignes And I make name ordaine and appoint my said Deare and Loving Wife Elizabeth Dann Sole and Only Executrix of this my last Will and Testament and no other In Witness whereof I the said John Dann the Testator to this my last Will and Testament in Writing have sett my hand and Seale this One and Twentieth Day of December Anno Dni 1720 And in the Seventh Yeare of the Reigne of our Sovereigne Lord George King of Great Brittaine &c.

Jno. Dann

Signed Sealed Published and declared by the said John Dann the Testator as and for his last Will and Testament the Day of the Date above written in the presence of us who have Subscribed our names as Witnesses thereunto in the presence of the said Testator

Thos. Harrison

John Smith

John Dann's will [17]

The lost portraits

The portraits of John and Eliza Dann were subsequently loss to history. The artist *Pieter van der Werff*, had learnt to paint from his brother Adriaen, both working during the *Dutch Golden Age.* Pieter spent most of his younger life in Rotterdam, painting the rich and famous. Overshadowed perhaps by his illustrious brother, in his thirties he travelled to England to seek commissions. We know he painted portraits for the Fairfax family and possibly the Duke of Marlborough, other works feature in private collections and public galleries. Over the centuries some have been sold, occasionally losing their original titles appearing at auctions simply as 'portraits of a man or woman'. Could these be the lost portraits of John and Eliza Dann?

c.1700 Pieter van der Werff (1665-1722) oils on canvas 48 x 40 cm

The fraudsters Brerewood & Pitkin

The fraudsters had fled abroad after the scandal, Pitkin was apprehended in Holland and Brerewood's creditors found him in Livorno Italy and hauled him back to stand trial.

Thomas Brerewood born around 1670 descended from a wealthy and prominent Chester family. Son of a vicar and a grandson of Sir Robert Brerewood, a justice on the Court of Common Pleas during the English Civil War. He was a member of the *Fishmongers' Company*, one of the most prestigious of the London Livery Companies.

Brerewood was the mastermind behind the massive fraud with his so called 'duped' partner Thomas Pitkin. They had plotted in the *Swan Tavern* in Cornhill in what became known as the 'Pitkin affair' of 1705. It caused the bankruptcy of *Coggs and Dann* five years later.

Brerewood was convicted in the London criminal court in March 1709, *"to be imprisoned for life in Newgate Prison and made to stand in the pillory three times each year"*...[18] – yet amazingly by November he had been freed on Queen Anne's pardon.

He was able to rebuild his fortune, ending his career in Maryland in the American Colonies as a respected man of substance and importance. In 1741, he became clerk of Baltimore County, a well-remunerated position which he held until his death in December 1746.

Thomas Pitkin was born in the village of Berkhamsted, Buckinghamshire in 1665. He came from a middle-class family, entering the trade of linen draper - wholesale cloth merchant. He married well, in fact several times. By 1693 Pitkin had received the freedom of the *Haberdashers Livery Company*, and had his shop at the sign of the *Black Spread Eagle* in Kings Street, Cheapside London.

Pitkin always blamed Brerewood, although they did have 'form' together. Some years earlier, both had been part of a scam known as the 'customs drawbacks system' whereby the unscrupulous could fraudulently recoup duty when they re-exported merchandise.

He had been detained in Amsterdam after a chance meeting with a creditor, the opportunistic William Luce. With the connivance of his Dutch agent Luce put him under house arrest and promptly sailed to England to acquaint the other creditors. However, he demanded a £200 reward and a percentage of the recovered estate for Pitkin's return.

Pitkin never made any restitution. He was able to move to the country, living in the small Essex village Belchamp Otten near Sudbury where he died in the summer of 1740 at the age of seventy-five. He is buried in the churchyard of St. Ethelbert and All Saints.

-4-

The attraction of piracy

"Yes, sir, they knew to be sure" [19]

For perspective, consider the career prospects, that between 1689 and 1740 the average wages for an ordinary sailor in the Royal Navy was 19s per month, or £12 7s per annum. However the seamen on the Spanish Expedition were contracted at £2 per month, £26 per annum.

As a pirate on the other hand, depending on how much was shared, a sum of £1,000 say, equalled roughly thirty-eight years of work, although capture could mean execution. Would it be worth the risk?

On arrival in Providence after returning from the Indian Ocean, roughly half of Every's pirates scattered to other Caribbean islands, the South American Portuguese colony of Bahia Brazil, and the North American colonies such as Philadelphia. Where it was rumoured, that Governor Markham had received £100 from each of Every's men who sort his protection. An example of how lax the colonial authorities were at that time is described as follows:

'Josiah Raynor landed at Long Island New York, with a chest containing over £1,000. A £50 bribe to Governor Benjamin Fletcher not only ensured his own protection, but also secured the return of the chest with its contents intact.' [20]

A smaller group who had sailed to the American colonies, set sail again in an un-named sloop together with the *Fancy's* boatswain Robert Prince. Arriving in Kinsale on the south east coast of Ireland in late August 1696, they promptly disappeared.

Out of the fifty or so crew that returned, only five were hanged. The *Sea flower* provided James Lewis arrested in Wapping and John Sparks, two more from the *Isaac,* Edward Forseith arrested in Newcastle and William Bishop in Exeter. William May the *Fancy's* steward (who had proposed a toast to Every's adventure on the eve of the Corunna mutiny) thought by sailing independently to Virginia, then taking passage to Bristol he could avoid attention. However journeying to London by coach he was arrested at the *White Lion* in Bath, subsequently tried and hanged. Hardly surprising, England had a highly developed network of spies and informers both male and female since Elizabethan times.

John Strousier and the boy seaman Robert Seely, from the *Sea Flower* settled in Ireland. Joseph Goss and Samuel Dawson were arrested but later released. Another, James Gragger made it to England, but after arrest in Norwich he too was released.

We know the young Phillip Middleton had been arrested in Dublin and John Dann later in Rochester, both turned King's Evidence, and were pardoned.

Joseph Dawson, one of the *Fancy's* quartermasters' captured in Yarmouth was due to be hanged but reprieved and pardoned the following year. The reformed pirate William Dampier (he had also sailed with the ill-fated 'Spanish Expedition' to Corunna and knew Every) had been a witness for the defence and also provided him with £20 bail. Some said Dawson was a government informer, because not only was he pardoned –but 'exempt from impressments in the Royal Navy'. A rare protection and highly sort after.

Despite the hue and cry, and whilst many pirates were arrested, most were released through insufficient evidence.

After being found guilty at the Old Bailey, and returned to Newgate prison, the men executed accounted for only about 10% of the estimated *Fancy's* crew that finally returned to Ireland and England.

The other 90% simply melted away, with up to £1,000 in their pockets. With odds like that, as John Dann aka Francis Danne, and John Avery, aka Henry Every, Long Ben, or perhaps Benjamin Bridgman would testify, it *was* worth the risk.

What became of Henry Every?

Twenty-four of his pirates were eventually captured, but only five hanged in London in November 1696. Yet 'Long Ben' eluded capture, vanishing from all records the same year.

In his statement to the authorities (the only detailed official record) John Dann says when he arrived in Dublin he heard "*Every was already there, although they did not meet,*" having travelled separately.

Testaments by two of his pirates confirmed as much, but were they truthful? Was Mrs Adams the new Mrs Bridgman, as Dann's chance meeting at the St Alban's coaching inn might indicate?

Perhaps Every also used the services of Madame Harache. The Huguenots with their secular broadmindedness and mercantile pragmatism had large communities in Holland, as well as The Cape and New Netherland in America.

Or did he seek out old acquaintance William Dampier -who was already in London, working on his journals titled 'A New Voyage Round the World' published the following year. A year earlier, Dampier had lost his claim in the High Court of the Admiralty for un-paid wages from the Spanish Expedition (£77 3s 6d) and probably short of money. It seems he was unaccountably sympathetic to many of Every's men; offering bail money to Joseph Dawson for example. We might speculate this was altruism, or secretly funded by Every? A few years later, in January 1699 in command of the *Roebuck* Dampier *(see image)* set sail on an Admiralty expedition to New Holland (Australia). On the journey south they arrived in Portuguese Bahia late March, staying a month. Whilst ashore he chanced upon some of Every's crew, John Guy the *Fancy's* carpenter, Broadneck his mate and Wastecoate but under various pretexts chose not to arrest them, much to the chagrin of his second-in-command, the chauvinistic lieutenant George Fisher. [21]

Dann also added to the 'smoke and mirrors' effect when he gave evidence by saying, *"Every and I landed in the north of Ireland at the end of June last, where we parted and Every went to Scotland. I heard that he was in Dublin when I was there, but did not see him. He had spoken of going to Exeter, being a Plymouth man."* [22] So we have Scotland, Dublin and the West Country, together with his name change, all adding to the confusion.

Unconfirmed accounts state Henry Every under an alias such as Benjamin Bridgman, or even Johnson had retired, quietly living out the rest of his life in either Britain or an unidentified tropical island. As the manhunt for him continued in the decade following his disappearance, sightings were frequently reported, but none proved reliable.

His death is variously reported in Barnstable or Bideford, but no evidence has been found. Some say he may have been a cousin of the well-known baronets of the same name, though this has not been proven conclusively. After the publication of Van Broeck's fictional memoir in 1709, which claimed he was ruling a pirate utopia in Madagascar, popular accounts increasingly took on a more legendary and romantic flavour.

Then much later in October 1781 John Knill the eccentric mayor of St Ives in Cornwall held a meeting with a descendant of Every who stated that, *"his father had told him that Captain Every, after wandering about in great poverty and distress, had died in Barnstaple, and was buried as a pauper".* [23] Again, repeating the usual confusing hearsay.

There were other factors in favour of Every's disappearance, nobody knew what name he was *actually* using, or importantly where he was heading. Thanks to the misleading evidence deliberate or otherwise by 'Mr Bridgman's accomplice', and repeated by others.

"Perhaps the greatest advantage the pirates had was the relative ease with which seamen could move from ship to ship, from port to port. The seafaring community of Europe and the colonies was huge and relatively fluid, making it easy for a man to 'lose' himself without too much difficulty provided he knew to keep his mouth shut and had a little bit of luck on his side." [24]

In truth, despite the unprecedented £1,000 reward no reliable information about Every, or a Mr Bridgman's whereabouts or activities ever emerged after June 1696 – He simply disappeared.

Every's fortune came in many forms. A widespread mixture of gold and silver coins; precious gemstones, silks and other fabrics, as well as tradable commodities like ivory.

The haul included Spanish silver coins known as 'pieces of eight', –as the fictional Long John's Silver's parrot would constantly squawk, and Arabic gold coins known as 'chaquins'. Gold and silver 'sequins' minted by the Republic of Venice, Portuguese gold and silver 'reals', and possibly a sprinkling of English gold 'sovereigns' and 'guineas too.

However, because the coins were literally 'worth their weight' they were frequently 'clipped' taking small pieces from each coin reducing their value, so they could be sold as bullion. This happened in the aftermath of the pirate raid whilst they were sharing the spoils.

It was commonly believed that gold was more universal than silver – so the crew of the *Fancy* readily agreed a gold for silver exchange with the crew of the *Pearl*. Outraged on discovering the gold coins had been 'clipped' the crew of the *Fancy* returned and retrieved their silver at gunpoint –going on to confiscate all *Pearl's* treasure.

However, Every did grant 2,000 pieces of eight to Captain Mace and his perfidious crew to buy provisions, then abandoned them to their fate.

"All of us had ample share of the treasure,
and used it wisely or foolishly, according to our natures."[25]

"...And when the fight was done we drank and this is what we said,

Here's to gentlemen at sea tonight, and a toast to all free men
And when the devil comes to take us home, he'll drink
With old Long Ben!"

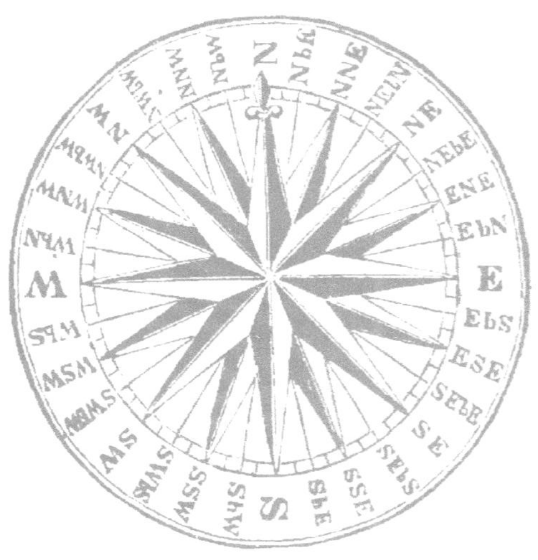

Timeline 1660 - 1722

1660c		-John Dann born East Hoathly Sussex
1662	28 August	-baptised Broomfield Kent, home village of mother Mary Deprose
1665-7	March-July	-Second Dutch War – *HMS Royal Charles* captured in the Medway
1670		-Father Thomas dies, John becomes sailor in the 'owling trade'
1672-4	April-Spring	-Third Dutch War
1679	May	-*Habeas Corpus Act* gains royal assent
1685	February	-*Charles II* dies his brother *James II* succeeds the throne
1688	September	-War against France, *James II* abdicates-flees into exile in France
	Winter	-Impressment by Royal Navy at *Mermaid Inn* Rye sent to Chatham becomes coxswain on *HMS Soldado*, a 16-gun fireship
1689	February	-The Glorious Revolution *William (of Orange) & Mary* invited to rule
	May	-*Soldado* takes part in the *Battle of Bantry Bay*
1690	July	-*Battle of Beachy Head (Henry Every –HMS Rupert)*
1693	Spring	-Leaves *Soldado* to join an expedition to the West Indies, signing on to the *James* then later the privateer *Charles II* of 46-guns
1694	May	- Joins Henry Every's mutiny in Corunna taking *Charles II* (re-named *Fancy)* and sails to the Indian ocean, to 'seek their fortune'
1695	September	-Attacks Grand Mughal's fleet ships *Fateh Muhammed, Ganj-i-sawai*
	November	-*Fancy* arrives Bourbon (Réunion Island) to share the spoils
1696	April	-Arrives Bahamas bribing Governor Trott, pirate crew disperse
	June	-Sails with Every to Ireland's west coast in the sloop *Sea Flower* travels to Dublin, returns via Holyhead and Chester to London
	July	-Arrives London meets with Huguenot émigré Anne Harache
		-Arrested at the *Bull Hotel* in Rochester Kent
	August	-Proclamation for the arrest of Henry Every, crew and accomplices £500 reward, the list omitted John Dann
	October	-First pirate trial Old Bailey, turns Kings Evidence
	November	-Second trial –five sentenced to death at Execution Dock Wapping
1697	December	-St Paul's Cathedral rebuilt by Wren after Great Fire, is consecrated
1698	August	-Summoned before the board of the *East India Company*
1699		-Joins John Coggs forming new partnership *Coggs & Dann*, goldsmith bankers at the sign of the *King's Head* in the Strand
1700	January	-Aged 40 marries Eliza - Elizabeth Noble
1705	February	-A bankruptcy fraud rocks London *(The Pitkin Affair*) implicating *Coggs and Dann*, with 217 named debts, totalling over £54,000
1707	May	-*Acts of Union,* uniting the parliaments of England and Scotland
1710	January	-*Coggs & Dann* declared bankrupt, announcement in *Post Man*
	March	-John Coggs dies
1712	June	-Government introduced the *Coggs' and Dann's Bill*
	November	-New play opens at *Drury Lane The Successful Pyrate* by Charles Johnson, depicting the life of Henry Every, it ran for several years
1713	April	-*Treaty of Utrecht* ends the *War of the Spanish Succession*
1714	August	-*Queen Anne* dies, George I succeeds
1722	August	-John dies in London age 56, Eliza follows four months later

Notes

[1] *Smuggling in Sussex*, Vol. X Sussex Archaeological Coll. 1857, page 231
[2] *Smuggling in the British Isles: A history*, Richard Platt, pages 111-112
[3] *Ibid*, page 112
[4] Jo Kirkham (Dr G. Mayhew), The Restoration 1689, *Ryemuseum.co.uk*
[5] *A Pirate of Exquisite Mind*, Diana & Michael Preston, pages 312-315
[6] *Jolly Roger*, Patrick Pringle, page 141
[7] *"Every offered Governor Nicholas Trott not only bribes in bullion and ivory but his entire ship, estimated at £50,000 (about 7 million dollars today)"*, Every and his men were welcomed by the Bahamian governor, and also dined at his house, *Pirate Nests and the Rise of the British Empire, 1570-1740,* Mark G. Hanna, page 192
[8] August 3 1696: Examination of John Dann, mariner, of Rochester, *Calendar of State Papers Colonial, America and West Indies*: Volume 15, December 1696, 11-20, Pages 248-267, 517. IV *www.british-history.ac.uk*
[9] August 4 1696: Narrative of Phillip Middleton of the ship *Charles Henry, (Fancy)* given to the Lords Justices of Ireland. *Calendar of State Papers:* Volume 15, December 1696, 11-20, Pages 248-267, 517, III *www.british-history.ac.uk*
[10] August 11 1698: Mr. Blackborne's (Secretary to the *East India Company*) letter of 8th, records *"an order for one Dann, lately Every's mate but pardoned, to attend the Board to-morrow"*, *Calendar of State Papers*: Volume 16: August 1698, 6-10, Pages 368-374 *www.british-history.ac.uk*
[11] Details revealed during the long subsequent bankruptcy hearings of Coggs & Dann in June 1710. *(sic)"…Danne hath allsoe in the name of Francis Danne the sum[m]e of £1300 Principall East India Stocke which he most humbly hopes his Creditors will not oblidge him to deliver up untill he has his full discharge & some reasionable allowance for the subsistance of him self & Family out of some part of his Estate…"* British Library records, Add. MS 38464, fols. 71r.-v
[12] *Banking: A short history*, Chase & Allen, page 36
[13] John and Martha Coggs (with un-married daughter Mary) are commemorated on a marble wall plaque in *St Mary's Church* Denham, Bucks.
[14] *The London Goldsmiths 1200-1800*, Sir Ambrose Heal, page 127
[15] *House of Lords Journal* Volume 19: 5 June 1712, Pages 468-469
[16] Eliza Dann's letter to William Draper Feb. 27, 1712 *n.s. British Library, Add. MS 38464, fol.192r*
[17] *London Metropolitan Archives*, Reg. of wills Microfilm reel 9051/12, fol 2
[18] *American Bankruptcy Law Journal*, Emily Kadens, Vol 84 2010, page 540
[19] *"Yes, sir, they knew for sure"* Dann's reply during the trial, when asked if the other defendants knew of the intention to mutiny, *King of the Pirates,* page 122
[20] *Ibid*, pages 110-111 [21] *Ibid*, page 150
[22] *Calendar of State Papers Colonial, America and West Indies*: Volume 15, December 1696, 11-20, Pages 248-267, 517. IV *www.british-history.ac.uk*
[23] *The Cornishman*, 24 October 1878, page 6 (Henry Every Wikipedia entry)
[24] *King of the Pirates,* E.T. Fox, page 119
[25] As Jim Hawkins recounts on last page, R. L. Stevenson's *Treasure Island*

Sources and acknowledgements

Dann family research through *genesreunited.co.uk* and *Ancestry.com*; *Ryemuseum.co.uk*; Henry Every's Wikipedia entry, his various biographies, particularly E.T. Fox; a personal thanks to Emily Kadens, who published *The Pitkin Affair: A Study of Fraud in Early English Bankruptcy,* and inadvertently alerted me to an ancestor. I have incorporated some of her extensive research, (gratefully acknowledged) from manuscripts of the *House of Lords*, *The National Archives* at Kew, *The British Library* in London and the *London Metropolitan Archives.* Further research –see bibliography, also Calendar of State Papers Colonial, America and West Indies, on line *www.british-history.ac.uk*

Relative currency comparisons and calculations*: www.measuringworth.com*

Poems and lyrics: *A Smuggler's Song, Puck of Pook's Hill, 1906,* courtesy of the National Trust, estate of Rudyard Kipling (1865-1936); *The Ballad of Long Ben* a popular shanty man song of the 1690s, source unknown (see also bibliography)
Images: cover & title page: pirates illustration from 1911 edition *Treasure Island*, courtesy of the estate of N.C.Wyeth (1882-1945), American artist and illustrator

Chapter 1: The smuggler: smuggling in the Romney Marshes, J.P.Smith engraving courtesy of *www.ryemuseum.co.uk;* East Hoathly parish church, courtesy *Wikipedia Commons;* Halland, East Hoathly *by Samuel Hieronymus Grimm 1783,* (Turner's Diary) courtesy *Sussex Archaeological Society; Mermaid Inn Rye,* Arthur Spencer etching c.1920 courtesy Grosvenor Prints, London, *Copyright F. & M. Ltd., Bedford*; The battle of Bantry Bay, *Wikipedia Commons*
Chapter 2: The pirate: Captain Every and the *Fancy*, *Wikipedia Commons*; The White Hart, St Albans, courtesy SAHAAS, *www.stalbanshistory.org;* The Swan with Two Necks Lad Lane, courtesy of *www.pubshistory.com*; White Bear coaching inn, Piccadilly courtesy *www.shadyoldlady.com*; Bull hotel Rochester courtesy of *www.dover-kent.com;* Old East India House Leadenhall Street, courtesy of *www.magnoliabox.com*
Chapter 3: The goldsmith banker: View of London from Southwark, (c.1630 *Dutch school), courtesy Museum of London;* St Botolph Bishopsgate by Alexander Poole Moore 1796, courtesy of *Sotheby's;* portraits of: Sir John Holt, Lord Chief Justice (1642–1710, John Churchill, 1st Duke of Marlborough (1650–1722), John Holles, 1st Duke of Newcastle (1662 –1711), Thomas Howard, 8th Duke of Norfolk, (1683–1732) Edward Henry Lee, 1st Earl of Lichfield (1663–1716) *Wikipedia Commons;* Major-General Henry Scott, 1st Earl of Deloraine, (1676–1730) courtesy *National Galleries of Scotland;* painting of John Coggs's estate, by *Jan Siberechts*, courtesy the *Tate Gallery London;* exterior of St Andrew's Church Holborn, courtesy of *london.lovesguide.com;* interior of St Andrew's Holborn courtesy of *www.british-history.ac.uk;* a print (c.1850) of Childs Banking House, Fleet Street, next to Temple Bar, courtesy of *www.ineartamerica.com* William Dampier, painting by Thomas Murray *1698, Wikipedia Commons,* Portraits of a lady & gentleman, (c.1700), Pieter van der Werff (1665-1722) unknown

Selected bibliography

BAER, Joel H. *Pirates of the British Isles,* Tempus Publishing, London 2005

COOPER, William Durrant, Esq., F.S.A. *Smuggling in Sussex,* Vol. X. of the Sussex Archaeological Collections, John Russell Smith, Soho Square 1857

CHASE, Franklin L, Allen, John K, *Banking: A short history*, Lanward Publishing Company, Chicago 1888

DANCY, J Ross, *Myth of the Press Gang: Volunteers, Impressment and the Naval Manpower Problem in the Late Eighteenth Century*, Boydell Press 2015

DOWNIE, Robert, *Who's Who in Davy Jones' Locker? A biographical directory of Pirates, Buccaneers and Privateers,* Southgate Books, Hereford

FOX, E.T., *King of the Pirates, The swashbuckling life of Henry Every*, The History Press, Stroud 2008

HANNA, Mark G., *Pirate Nests and the Rise of the British Empire, 1570-1740,* University of North Carolina Press 2015

HEAL, Sir Ambrose, (compiled by), *The London Goldsmiths 1200-1800,* Worshipful Company of Goldsmiths, Cambridge University Press 1935

HILTON PRICE, F.G., *A Handbook of London Bankers, some of their Predecessors, the Early Goldsmiths 1677-1876*, Chatto & Windus, Piccadilly 1876

KADENS, Emily *'The Pitkin Affair: A Study of Fraud in Early English Bankruptcy',* Baker and Botts Professor in Law, *University of Texas School of Law*, Austin (since 2013, *Northwestern Pritzker School of Law*, Chicago), published in American Bankruptcy Law Journal, Vol. 84, 2010, pages 483-570

McCOOEY, Christopher, *Smuggling on the South Coast,* Amberley Publishing, Stroud 2012

PLATT, Richard, *Smuggling in the British Isles: A history*, The History Press 2011

PRESTON, Diana & Michael, *A Pirate of Exquisite Mind –The Life of William Dampier,* Corgi Books 2005

PRINGLE, Patrick, *Jolly Rodger, The Story of the Great Age of Piracy*, Dover Publications Inc., New York 2001

SCOULOUDI, Irene, Ed. *Huguenots in Britain & their French Background 1550-1800*, Macmillan Press, London 1987

A pirate in the family

The protagonist of this story has no known direct descendants. Family connections are traced through his uncle William, and follows one particular descending paternal line - through fifteen reigns *Charles I to George VI*

Reigns of Elizabeth I & James I 1558-1625

Jasper Dann *b.1593 Heathfield, Sussex*	*m. 1621 East Hoathly Sussex*	*Anne Bonnicke b. c1600 East Hoathly Sussex d. 1632 Sussex*	*4 Children:* **William** *b.1625, John 1628,* **Thomas** *1631, Soloman 1632*

Reigns of Charles I (Interregnum) & Charles II 1625-1685

William Dann *1625-1670 b.& d. East Hoathly Sussex m. 1675 Mary Durrant 1655-1690? b.Heathfield, Sussex 3 children: Grace 1676-, John 1678-,* ***William 1690***	***Thomas Dann*** *1631-1670, b.&d. East Hoathly Sussex m. 14 Feb 1655 Mary Deprose b. 1635? Kent, d.? 4 Children?: Katherine, Sarah, Ann ?* ***John Dann*** *b. c1660 East Hoathly Sussex, baptised 28 August 1662 Kent, d.1722 London, smuggler, sailor, pirate & goldsmith banker m. 1700 Elizabeth Noble 1661-1722 in London (no children?) (also went under the alias of Francis Danne)*

Reigns of James II & William & Mary 1685-1702

William Dann *b. 1690 Warbleton, Sussex d. 1766 Watling, Sussex*	*m.1712 Dallington, Sussex*	*Mary Ticehurst b. 1690 Warbleton, Sussex, d. 1770 Burwash, Sussex 10 children: Jasper 1713, Hannah 1714, Mary 1715 (twin), George 1715 (twin),* ***John 1717****, Hannah 1718, William 1719 (twin), James 1719 (twin), Mary 1722 (twin), Thomas 1722 (twin)*

Reigns of Anne, George I & II 1702-1760

John Dann *1717-1802 b.Burwash, Sussex*	*m.1753 Wartling Sussex*	*Frances Ford 1734-? b.Herstmonceaux, Sussex 10 children: John 1767, David 1768, Joseph 1769,* ***Jesse 1771****, Abraham 1775, Francis, 1777, Mary 1779, Hannah 1781, Peter 1783, Ruth 1785*

Reigns of George III, IV & William IV 1760-1837

Jesse (John) Dann *married 1794* *Rhoda Glazier*
1771-1844
b. Battle, E Sussex d. Hailsham, Sussex

Rhoda Glazier c 1776-1850, b & d. Battle, E Sussex
*1 child? **John 1816,***

John Dann *1st marriage c 1839* *Elizabeth Meads*
c 1816-1870
b. Battle, E Sussex

Elizabeth Meads b.1816, d.1840 (childbirth?)
1 child: Mary 1840,

John Dann *2nd marriage 1856 St Leonards, E. Sussex* *Arabella Fuller*
c 1816-1870
b. Battle, E Sussex
gamekeeper
d. Hollington, E. Sussex

*Arabella Fuller 1837-1893, b. Fairlight, Hastings, E. Sussex, laundress, d. Hastings Sussex (related to 'Mad Jack' Fuller 1757–1834, Sussex squire, politician, philanthropist) 6 children: **Ernest 1857**, Frank 1858, Nelson 1860, Mary 1863, Emily 1867, Benjamin 1870*
(Arabella's 2nd marriage to William Woods in 1875)

Reigns of Victoria & Edward VII 1837-1910

Ernest John Dann *Married 1885 Hailsham Sussex* *Fanny Lottie Isabella Russell*
b.1857 Hastings, Sussex
general labourer-brickmaker (journeyman),
d. 1935 Dover?

Fanny Lottie Isabella Russell b.1867 Hastings, E. Sussex, Laundress, d.1951? Dover Kent
*8 children: Emily 1886, Albert 1888, Florence 1890, Nelson 1892, **William 1894,** Fanny 1896, James 1898, Annie 1900*

William John Dann *Lived with c.1919 Dover & Hastings* *Rosie Allum (m. John Robertson 1917- who deserted her the following year)*
b 1894 Arlington, Sussex,
soldier, labourer,
d. 1976 Hastings

Rosie Allum b. 1895 Hastings Sussex, laundress, d. 1979 Hastings
4 children: John Albert (Jack) 1917, Bill 1920, Betty 1921, May 1927

Reign of George V & Edward VIII 1910-1936

John (Jack) Albert Dann	*William (Bill) Richard James Dann*	*Elizabeth (Betty) Florence Dann*	*Dorothy (May) Dann*
Adopted 1917-1943	*1920-after 1956?*	*1921-1996*	*1927-1998*
sailor Royal Navy,	*m. Louisette ? c.1947*	*m. Harry Barrett 1942*	*m. Tommy Bristow 1946*
m. Lena Morgan 1942	*1 child*	*2 children*	*3 children*
1 child			

Reign of George VI 1936-1952

Robert John Dann	*[4] Christiane b.1948*	*[2] Sandra b. 1947*	*[3] Carol b.1947*
[1] b.1943		*[7] Dawn b.1961*	*[5] Martin b.1949*
			[6] Graham b.1952
First cousin five times removed	*Fourth cousin five times removed*	*Second & seventh cousins five times removed*	*Third, fifth, sixth cousins five times removed*

Reign of Elizabeth II 1952-

…and this is where the 'Dann' name of this cadet branch of Mr Bridgman's Accomplice begins to disappear

Author

John Dann, was born in Wales worked in London, and lived in Sussex for many years. He served for a short time in the Royal Navy, as did his father before him; continuing the link with Sussex and the sea.
Like his namesake has also cruised the 'Babs' and Indian Ocean now spends his time writing, sailing the *Magatha* and beachcombing with his Labrador in Cornwall.

Other books

Struck by Lightning (2012)
A sailor's first-hand story about a Second World War fighting ship
HMS Lightning 1941–1943 (with Eric Gilroy)
(Paperback)

Thomas Cook's Rugby Club (2013)
Its life and times 1910-1966
(Paperback, revised Hardback edition 2018)

Maud Coleno's Daughter (2017)
The life of Mayfair hostess Dorothy Hartman 1898-1957
(Hardback)

Rugger Shorts (2017)
Reflections on the amateur game -An anthology of rugby trivia
(Paperback)

A Welsh Uncle (2018)
Memories of Tom Morgan 1898 – 1957
(Paperback)

…perhaps a glimpse of Mr Bridgman's accomplice?

ND - #0161 - 080726 - C41 - 234/156/2 - PB - 9781784566364 - Gloss Lamination